THE LITTLE BOOK OF

THOMAS HARDY

Written by Emily Wollaston

THE LITTLE BOOK OF

THOMAS HARDY

Written by Emily Wollaston

This edition first published in the UK in 2008
by Green Umbrella Publishing

© Green Umbrella Publishing 2008

www.gupublishing.co.uk

Publishers Jules Gammond and Vanessa Gardner

Printed and bound in China

ISBN 978-1-906229-60-3

The views in this book are those of the author but they are general views only and readers are urged to consult the relevant and qualified specialist for individual advice in particular situations.

Green Umbrella Publishing hereby exclude all liability to the extent permitted by law of any errors or omissions in this book and for any loss, damage or expense (whether direct or indirect) suffered by a third party relying on any information contained in this book.

All our best endeavours have been made to secure copyright clearance for every photograph used but in the event of any copyright owner being overlooked please address correspondence to Green Umbrella Publishing, The Old Bakehouse, 21 The Street, Lydiard Millicent, Swindon SN5 3LU

Contents

The Life of Thomas Hardy

The landscape between Puddletown to the east of Dorchester, on the edge of Thorncombe Wood, was the setting chosen by stonemason, John Hardy, who built a house there in around 1800 on the Kingston Maurward estate. With his wife Mary, Hardy began the family business of masonry and bricklaying and had six children who were brought up in the house, including two sons named Thomas. The elder Thomas died unexpectedly in 1837 and the younger took over the business from his mother, who by then had been widowed, some years later while she continued to manage the company accounts. In 1839, Thomas married Jemima Hand, who was already pregnant with their first child. On 2 June 1840, their son, Thomas Hardy, was born in an upstairs bedroom in the area known as Higher Bockhampton in Dorset in the parish of Stinsford.

At first, the doctor delivering the baby was convinced that the infant was stillborn, but the quick actions of the attending midwife showed the baby was very much alive. However, Hardy was somewhat of a sickly child and was kept at home until he was eight years of age. His health and general well-being were a cause of worry for his parents. He was followed by three siblings: Mary, born in 1841, Henry, born 10 years later in 1851 and Katherine, known as Kate, in 1856. Jemima Hardy had worked in domestic service but was keen for her first-born son to prosper. While Henry was trained in the family business, Mary and Kate trained as school teachers. The family were reasonably well off, but came from a humble background. Hardy's mother introduced her son to the countryside and encouraged him to find a passion for books. Hardy's grandmother, Mary, would sit with the family by the fire during the evenings and tell them stories.

Hardy would become one of the most renowned and well-loved writers of all time who wrote during the period that united the Victorian and modern eras of literature. Sometimes described as dour, Hardy had a gift for writing about the pain of human suffering in his novels and the eternal struggle for life. But it was not as a

LEFT & ABOVE
The Dorset landsape was the setting for most of Hardy's work

CLASSIC LITERATURE

novelist that Hardy had meant to make his living or share his passion. His career had begun as a poet and Hardy once commented that he would never have written a line of prose if his poems had received more recognition. However, novels such as *The Mayor Of Casterbridge, Jude The Obscure* and *Tess Of The d'Urbervilles* are some of the titles for which he is best remembered.

The young Hardy learnt to play the violin and developed a love of music. Taught by his father, who – like his own father – was an accomplished church musician, Hardy toured the local countryside playing for weddings and dances. It is surely the impressions of rural life he encountered that contributed so widely to his writing about people and places where he drew from personal knowledge and experience. His mother was well read and an ambitious woman who guided her son's formal education and supplemented it when it ended when Hardy turned 16 years of age. He had attended the school established by Julia Augusta Martin in Stinsford during 1848 and then spent a year studying at the British School in Dorchester. His education continued at a commercial academy run by Isaac Last where Hardy was able to study Latin. When his years of schooling ended in 1856, Hardy was apprenticed to Dorchester architect John Hicks.

It was in that same year that Hardy witnessed the hanging of Elizabeth Martha Browne, a woman condemned to death for the murder of her husband. She had caught John Browne, 20 years her junior, in bed with another woman and had brought a wood axe down on his scull when he'd taken his whip to her following an argument. Despite the public sympathy that Browne received as a result of the abuse she'd suffered at the hands of her husband, the fact that until almost the last she claimed he had died from a kick from a horse meant the home secretary felt powerless to grant a reprieve. It would be more than another 100 years before the legal system would bring in diminished responsibility so Browne became the last woman to be publicly hanged in Dorset. This experience is said to have influenced

LEFT Workers from the countryside inspired Hardy

CLASSIC LITERATURE

ABOVE Lulworth Cove or Lustead Cove as Hardy referred to it

RIGHT Public hangings had a profound effect on Hardy and his writings

the fate of the character Tess in *Tess Of The d'Urbervilles*. It was an event that struck deeply within Hardy – he still wrote about it when in his 80s. Two years later he attended the last public hanging in Dorset, also outside Dorchester prison, of James Seale who was executed for the murder of Sarah Guppy. Public hangings were abolished by law in 1868.

During his early years as an apprentice to John Hicks, and later as an assistant, Hardy is known to have thought seriously about attending university and entering the church, but for whatever reason, he decided against this route and in 1862 he went to London to gain more experience as an architect in the offices of Arthur Blomfield. It was here that he continued writing the poetry that had gripped him since 1861. He tried a number of publishers but all works were returned to a disappointed Hardy. He kept many of these poems and spent many hours discussing modern thought with his friend and mentor, Horace Moule. They had become friends when the architect was apprenticed in Dorchester and it was the vicar's son from Fordington who encouraged the young Hardy to write poetry. Moule was also instrumental in helping the aspiring poet to further his studies while around the same time Hardy began to teach himself Greek with the help of dialect poet William Barnes.

CLASSIC LITERATURE

ABOVE Hardy spent much time studying paintings at the National Gallery

While in London, Hardy regularly went to the opera and even joined a choir. He was also keen to study the paintings in the National Gallery – which he documented in a notebook – and began a course on English Poets. His first published work, *How I Built Myself A House*, was a small satirical sketch. Receiving £3 15 shillings, Hardy's work was published in *Chambers' Journal*. He began a short-lived romance with Eliza Nicholls, who worked as a lady's maid, but the affair was over by the time he returned to Dorchester to work once again for John Hicks in 1867. The following year he completed his first novel, *The Poor Man And The Lady* which, today, is sadly lost and unpublished. The novel, Hardy was advised, shouldn't be published as it would offend the genteel Victorian audience. The book was rejected by publishers due to its overtly satirical nature and much of it was then destroyed by the author. He followed the novel with a second, *Desperate Remedies*, but this too was unsuccessful, despite having a plot; Hardy had been advised that a plot was essential.

Meanwhile, when John Hicks died in 1869 his business was taken over by Gerald Crickmay, specialists in church restoration, who, in 1870, sent Hardy to Boscastle in north Cornwall to restore the parish church of St Juliot. Emma Lavinia Gifford (1840-1912) was the sister-in-law of the vicar of St Juliot and she and 30-year-old Hardy quickly fell in love despite his feelings for his cousin. Hardy had had a brief fling with his beautiful and highly independent cousin Tryphena Sparks who was hoping to become a teacher. Gifford, however, was keen to encourage his writing and the couple were married in 1874 even though the bride's family did not approve of the union. Hardy's family also did not attend the wedding. But Hardy's return to his old job (even though he was writing) had also brought him great sadness when the year before, in 1873, his lifelong friend Horace Moule committed suicide at the age of 41. It was writing that kept Hardy from falling into a deep depression over the tragedy.

Just prior to these events, *Desperate Remedies* was eventually published anonymously by William Tinsley in 1871. It was set in three volumes and Hardy had had to guarantee the cost of the printing. The *Morning Post* and the *Athenaeum* both gave favourable reviews of the novel which encouraged Hardy to offer *Under The Greenwood Tree* to Tinsley in 1872. The reviews were enthusiastic and Hardy continued with his next novel, *A Pair Of Blue Eyes* which was in the early stages of composition while he courted his future wife. Tinsley asked Hardy to write a serial

CLASSIC LITERATURE

ABOVE Athelstan, King of Wessex

for his magazine – a usual publishing venture in the Victorian era – and the budding author was further excited by the offer from renowned editor, Leslie Stephen, to write a serial for the influential *The Cornhill* magazine. He was also writing *Far From The Madding Crowd* by this time, which helped him come to terms with Moule's untimely death. The year of 1873 also saw the publication of *A Pair Of Blue Eyes* which drew on the courtship of his wife. It was the first novel published in the author's own name.

When *Far From The Madding Crowd* was published, the same year as he and Emma Gifford married, Hardy properly used the semi-imaginary county of Wessex for the first time. Wessex was originally the ancient kingdom of the West Saxons, ruled by King Alfred the Great, between 871-899. The boundaries of Wessex had expanded and contracted over 10 centuries as wars reigned and with its capital at Winchester, the large part of the county lay firmly in the south west of England. Although King Alfred did much to advance the development of the English monarchy, it was during the reign of King Athelstan (925-939) that the royal house of Wessex reached its peak and the Wessex king laid claim to the title "King of all Britain". Hardy used his own imaginary Wessex and moved buildings and places to best serve his plot, not because he wanted to allude that these things were not real, but rather because he wanted his readers to understand that the novels were fictional.

Far From The Madding Crowd was also Hardy's first commercial success and, despite having a good job with Gerald Crickmay, he abandoned architecture in

ABOVE Maxgate, Hardy's home

pursuit of a different career…as a novelist. Over the next 25 years, Thomas Hardy wrote 10 further novels.

Following a honeymoon in Paris, Thomas and Emma Gifford Hardy moved between various rented accommodation in London, Yeovil and then to Sturminster Newton where he wrote *The Return Of The Native* (1878), and finally to Max Gate, a house on the outskirts of Dorchester. It would be the couple's last move. The house was designed by Hardy and built by his brother Henry and it was here that the literary genius wrote *The Mayor Of Casterbridge* (1886), *The Woodlanders* (1887) and *Tess Of The d'Urbervilles* (1891) which received criticism for its sympathetic portrayal of a "fallen woman". In 1895, *Jude The Obscure* followed and gained just

CLASSIC LITERATURE

ABOVE Hardy was very
fond of the traditional
way of life that was
slowly disappearing

as much, if not more criticism, than its predecessor due to its overtly frank treatment of sex which brought about outcries from the repressed Victorian society.

Hardy and his wife were going through a difficult patch in their marriage and the publication of *Jude* further compounded their differences when Mrs Hardy became concerned that *Jude The Obscene* as it was sometimes referred to could be taken as autobiographical for its attack on the institution of marriage. Such was the public outcry that many bookshops and booksellers sold copies neatly packaged inside brown paper bags. However, by this time, Hardy had become highly celebrated as an author and he was so disgusted by the reaction to his two greatest novels that he put down his writing pen.

Along with the novels, Hardy also wrote a collection of renowned short stories between 1871 and 1895 which reflected both his fondness for the traditional way of rural life – of which he had been familiar as a child – and the new undercurrents of change that were threatening to sweep right through the Victorian era. First there were social problems connected to innovations in agriculture, and the railways were fast gaining in momentum. The industrial revolution was also making waves and quickly changing the face of the English countryside while Hardy himself was equally concerned with the hypocrisy and unfair attitudes towards sexual behaviour at the turn of the century.

Put in simplistic terms, Hardy painted a vivid picture of rural life throughout the 19th century which celebrated both the joys and the suffering of a harsh reality. His main characters and protagonists were rarely accepted by the societies in which they lived and once on the outside, were very often kept there both by their own actions and by those around them. Hardy's novels are full of injustice and alienation and he was adept at emphasising the negative powers of fate and the impersonal way in which working class people were treated in his stories. His

ABOVE The idyllic sort of life that so appealed to Hardy

works were full of crises and angst where, due to the social morals and thinking at the time, little could be done to turn about events or change the landscape of enduring fate. Victims were dealt with harshly and emotions were drawn out painfully and irrevocably. Inhumane and uncaring attitudes were sketched and moulded exquisitely by Hardy.

Although Hardy openly preferred his verse to his prose, he continued with the novels as a way to earn a living. Early on he had been content to write his novels

CLASSIC LITERATURE

to the requirements of magazine editors who were keen to serialise them in their publications. The serialised versions of both *Tess* and *Jude* had had the more "obscene" or risqué chapters cut or amended to fit with Victorian magazine etiquette. Thrills and excitement were a prerequisite and Hardy was well aware he must not offend the female readership. But his style would come to develop and his attitude for stories that could be serialised was changing and for the book versions of *Tess* and *Jude,* cut chapters and amended prose were reinstated. Short in stature – Hardy was just over five feet tall – but tall in social standing, the novelist began to herald fame and fortune, despite some public criticism, and he became acquainted with the higher echelons of Victorian society. Many critics believe that Hardy's greatest works contained characteristically awkward prose and an overuse of coincidences, but this could also be applied to lesser known novels such as *The Trumpet Major* (1880) and *A Laodicean* (1881) which was written when the author was ill in bed. Hardy had dealings with poet Robert Browning, Alfred, Lord Tennyson and with the poet and essayist Matthew Arnold to name but a few. He was also close friends with T E Lawrence whose departure for India in 1927 greatly saddened the author. He enjoyed travelling to Germany, France and Italy and had a good life, but his relationship with Emma Gifford Hardy was seemingly under increasing strain.

However, Hardy would not describe himself as a pessimist either in his novels (despite appearances) or in his personal life. He was fiercely private, but was happy to divulge that he believed that man can live with a degree of happiness if he is prepared to understand and accept his place in the universe. He read Charles Darwin and agreed with the theory of evolution. However, although Hardy had given up Christianity, his religious beliefs fell somewhere between being agnostic and spiritual.

After the outcries brought about by the publication of *Tess Of The d'Urbervilles* and *Jude The Obscure*, Hardy turned his attentions once again to poetry. Most of his poetry had lain unpublished until 1898 when *Wessex Poems* were unleashed, followed by *Poems Of The Past And Present* in 1902. He also published *The Dynasts*, a huge drama of the Napoleonic Wars where all the characters appear as puppets who have their actions determined by the "Immanent Will". This was a philosophy that Hardy believed in. Although not highly optimistic, the Immanent Will, is the belief that a blind force drives the universe and in the distant future it may see and understand itself, giving some room for hope. All in all, *The Dynasts* comprised of 19 acts and 130 scenes and was published in three parts in 1903, 1905 and 1908. The drama was intended to be read – never acted – and has often been referred to as Hardy's masterpiece published by Macmillan. He also continued to publish shorter verse and in 1914, his most famous volume of poems *Satires Of Circumstance* was published. In 1910, the same year he was awarded the Order of Merit, Hardy was given the freedom of the borough of Dorchester, however, he had previously refused a knighthood. Hardy and Emma Gifford Hardy were estranged at the time of her death in 1912, and

LEFT British soldier, adventurer and author Thomas Edward Lawrence

ABOVE Cambridge University

Hardy struggled greatly with his wife's passing. It is known that he wished he could have understood her more before she died and it is well documented that much of his poetry from 1912 on was written as a huge outpouring of grief for the loss of his wife. The couple had become estranged during 1898 and kept themselves separate at Max Gate.

The previous decade had been particularly tough for Hardy. His mother, Jemima Hardy, "the single most important influence" in his life, died in 1904, his father having died 12 years earlier in 1892. But in 1905, he met Florence Emily Dugdale who would become his assistant and secretary before becoming his wife in 1914. Dugdale was 40 years his junior and quite upset by her new husband's continual outpouring of grief in his poetry for his first wife. At the outbreak of World War I, Hardy committed himself to writing for the Allied forces when he joined a group of writers aiming to provide solace and comfort for all those involved in the war effort. Then, in 1915, his sister Mary died while his distant cousin Frank was killed at Gallipoli.

Hardy continued to write until the end of his life. He worked on his autobiography between 1920 and 1927 which was disguised as the work of Florence Hardy. Published in two volumes, the work was made public in 1918 and 1930. He was honoured by Doctorates of Literature from Cambridge University in 1913 and Oxford University in 1920. He died on 11 January 1928 at the age of 88 at his home in Max Gate, Dorchester. There was some disagreement over where the renowned writer should be buried and eventually a compromise was reached. It was decided that Hardy's heart should be buried in Emma Gifford Hardy's grave in Stinsford, while his ashes were interred at Westminster Abbey in Poets Corner. There is an unconfirmed rumour that Hardy's housekeeper carelessly left his heart in the author's kitchen which was then consumed by a cat. A pig's heart was then supposedly placed in the grave of his first wife. No-one knows for sure whether this story is true and biographies, writings and documentaries about Hardy's life make little or no reference to the rumour. Thomas Hardy remained close to his brother and two sisters throughout his life. His brother, Henry also died in 1928. Interestingly, none of the Hardys had any children and the family line died with Kate Hardy in 1940.

It has always been difficult to excel in any literature genre, but Hardy was a rare and gifted man who managed to secure his name in two: as a poet and a novelist. He achieved greatness in both fields and became a quiet and lasting influence on both poets and novelists alike in the modern literary era. Some argue that not many people read Hardy these days other than scholars and students, but maybe that's misguided. J D Scott, the literary editor of *The Spectator* coined the term "The Movement" in 1954 to describe a group of writers that included Hardy alongside Larkin, Amis and Elizabeth Jennings to name but some. The Movement was essentially English and was a reaction to the extreme romanticism of the New Apocalyptics of the previous major movement in British poetry.

The last book to be published in Hardy's lifetime was *Human Shows* in 1925. *Winter Words* was published posthumously in 1928. *The Early Life Of Thomas Hardy* and *The Later Years Of Thomas Hardy* were both published in Florence Hardy's name.

BELOW Hardy's ashes were placed in Poet's Corner at Westminster Abbey

CLASSIC LITERATURE

Hardy Country

Hardy stated that "…this is an imaginative Wessex only" when describing the semi-imaginary country that he used to set the plots for his novels. However, he went to painstaking lengths to ensure that places were named appropriately and accurately. It did not take shape in its final format until well into the later novels. Wessex evolved over time in size and how he imagined his county might look. It was eventually unified for all his novels and poems.

In 1884 when writing *The Mayor Of Casterbridge*, Wessex began to take its more final form and the town of Casterbridge was actually based on Dorchester in his beloved Dorset while Weymouth, for example, became Budmouth. From the 1890s, the Dorset landscape which provided the backdrop to Hardy's novels began attracting the readership. Hardy had collaborated with Hermann Lea to produce a definitive guide, first published in 1913, to *Thomas Hardy's Wessex*. The book was reprinted with the title *Highways And Byways In Hardy's Wessex* in 1925, 1969 and finally in 1978. Many of the novel's settings occur around the attractive thatched cottage in which Hardy was born at Higher Bockhampton. In his writing, the place is known as Mellstock and was the main setting for *Under The Greenwood Tree*. In *Far From The Madding Crowd*, the town of Puddletown was renamed Weatherbury. In *Tess*, the Vale of Little Dairies is named after Blackmore while the River Frome is also used as a landscape backdrop named "Vale of the Great Dairies".

CLASSIC LITERATURE

The Hardy Cottage was vacated by the family in 1911, when Henry, Mary and Kate moved to another house built by Henry on the other side of the Frome Valley. Several tenants then occupied the property before it was eventually returned to the Kingston Maurward estate and subsequently bought by a local farmer. The National Trust acquired the property in 1948 and opened the former birthplace of one of the greatest writers of the modern era to the public. To the front of the house are three upstairs windows. The middle room was the bedroom of Thomas and Jemima Hardy and the room in which Hardy was born. To the left was the room shared by Mary and Kate, to the right, the bedroom that Thomas Hardy and Henry shared.

Today, what was the kitchen is now an office while the narrow entrance leads into the parlour which was the principal room of the house. The low ceiling is beamed as it would have been during Hardy's time. The parlour housed a large open fireplace and originally, the front door was opposite to the front of the building. Towards the back of the cottage is a small room called the "office". It is thought that Hardy's father and grandfather would have kept their money in this room and prepared their accounts. In fact, there are still bars on the window. From what was Hardy's bedroom window it is possible to see the monument to Admiral Thomas Masterman Hardy (a distant relative) found on Blackdown Hill when winter removes the leaves from the west facing trees. During the time that Hardy lived in the cottage it was approached by a dirt track along which there were around eight cottages with large families of 30 or more housed in them. The Hardy family were lucky to have so few people in their own living space. Class played a big part in society and there was minimal interaction between the self-employed artisans and craftsmen and the labourers and field hands. Within this small community the Hardys enjoyed a form of superior social status.

The garden was utilised by the Hardy family to its full extent and was their mainstay for vegetables. It meant they could be mainly self-supporting growing

LEFT Hardy was inspired and influenced by the landscape

CLASSIC LITERATURE

ABOVE The unique lanscape of valleys and heaths

carrots, onions, parsnips, beans, potatoes and peas. During the autumn, the pig – which had been fattened during the summer – was slaughtered and salted while apples were harvested from the trees and beehives were kept. Life was lived according to the season and the cyclical calendar of the church where major highlights included Easter, Whitsun and Christmas. Markers during the year consisted of lambing season, haymaking and harvest and social activities were provided in the form of weddings, dances and Christmas parties. The church of St Michael at Stinsford is where Hardy was baptized. Much of the church dates from the early 13th century and it was here that Hardy's heart was buried on 16 January 1928. The south aisle window is a memorial to Hardy designed by Douglas Strachan in 1930.

CLASSIC LITERATURE

Dorchester was known intimately to Hardy and many of his writings encapsulates the ancient town. For example, the King's Arms Hotel, built in the 19th century, is used a great deal in his novels. The bow window to the front, overhanging the front door, was where Michael Henchard took up his position as Mayor of Casterbridge. Today, the Dorset County Museum houses a comprehensive collection of Hardy artefacts including manuscripts and personal items and there is even a reconstruction of the author's study. Hardy was particularly interested in the museum and he became a frequent visitor.

When Hardy was growing up, however, Dorchester was a market town and the county town of Dorset. There were around 6,500 people living in the area during the mid 1800s and despite being small had a number of banks, shops and bookstores as well as a prison, a hospital, county courts, a museum and a workhouse. Trading was done at the Saturday market and everyone thronged to the high street. When Hardy was seven years old, the railway reached Dorchester and gave the town a connection to London.

BELOW Dorchester the county town of Dorset

However, sophisticated progress was relatively slow and stagecoaches were still infinitely more popular than steam locomotives. There were also two barracks for infantry and artillery in Dorchester and uniformed men were a common sight in the town of Hardy's youth. It was also common during his formative years for local men to roll barrels of blazing tar down the steep streets (a tradition that was finally brought to a halt in the late 1870s). It was a West Country tradition that would continue unabated

CLASSIC LITERATURE

elsewhere though. Living alongside the large numbers of the middle classes in Dorset were large numbers of poor people who lived mainly in the area of Fordington. Lower Fordington, along the banks of the River Frome had become an overcrowded urban slum during the latter part of the 19th century and became infamous in Hardy's novels as Mixen Lane (known in real life as Mill Street).

Known as the "booziest place in Dorset", because of its brewery and several inns during Hardy's time, Marnhull was named by Hardy as Marlott for *Tess Of The d'Urbervilles* where the protagonist of the novel was born and raised. Shaftesbury (or Shaston as it's known in *Tess*) is about six miles north east of Marnhull. And, in the valley of the Frome River, (Valley of the Great Dairies), Tess meets Angel Clare with whom she falls in love. The Turbeville window in the church of St John the Baptist (dating from around the late 16th century) in Bere Regis is dedicated to the family whose name inspired Hardy for the d'Urbervilles while the town itself is named Kingsbere in the novel. Stonehenge on Salisbury Plain in Wiltshire is where Tess has managed to live three idyllic days with Angel Clare before she is arrested for the murder of her former husband – the man who ruined her.

Puddletown is the Weatherbury of Hardy's Wessex and features prominently in *Far From The Madding Crowd*. Here Hardy had many relatives on both his mother's and father's side of the family and it was not uncommon for him to walk across the heath from Bockhampton to visit. St Mary's church is featured a great deal in the novel and its oldest parts date from about 1200. The interior, even today, is pure 17th century and the impressive west gallery was built in 1635. During Hardy's youth, Puddletown was a busy, well populated village (verging on a small town) and was known as Piddletown after the River Piddle on the banks of which the village sits. At the end of the late 1850s there were seven shops, three bakers, two butchers, two tailors, two dressmakers, a grocer, six boot and shoe makers, a surgeon and a dentist – not bad for a village environment. There were also three blacksmiths, three

CLASSIC LITERATURE

stonemasons and two school teachers. The village carrier went to Dorchester on a Wednesday and Saturday according to Post Office records and the mail cart delivered to the Post Office each morning. There were two inns and two beer houses who served the many artisans and craftsmen that lived in the area who in turn served the surrounding farming community. Hardy's uncle, James Sparks, who married Maria, Jemima Hardy's sister, had a lively household and lived in a house known as Sparks Corner with his wife, three daughters and two sons (Tryphena Sparks was born later in 1851). These cousins were firm favourites with the young Hardy who was particularly taken with his attractive older cousin Martha and he enjoyed special friendships with James and Nathaniel Sparks. Later, between 1867 and 1870 there was a great deal of speculation about Hardy and the attractive 16-year-old Tryphena Sparks.

Thomas Hardy senior was involved in the restoration of Athelhampton House, located about a mile east of Puddletown. Dating from about 1485, it was here that Hardy's cousin Tryphena taught at the school which was found in the grounds. It was a place that

Hardy would visit often during his formative years. And, in the village of Upwey, between Weymouth (Hardy's Budmouth) and Dorchester is The Old Ship Inn where Dick Dewy proposed to Fancy Day as they travelled to Mellstock (Bockhampton) in *Under The Greenwood Tree*. Shaston, or Shaftesbury, is the main setting for *Jude The Obscure* while Corfe Castle is transformed into Corvsgate Castle of Hardy's Wessex. Salisbury – where Hardy visited often – was renamed Melchester in Wessex.

ABOVE Corfe Castle in Dorset

LEFT St Marys Church Puddletown

CLASSIC LITERATURE

Although not a "City person", Hardy did spend quite some time in London where he was first employed by Arthur Blomfield at 9 St Martin's Place, just off Trafalgar Square. Hardy found lodgings north of Kensington Gardens at 3 Clarence Place but moved to 16 Westbourne Park Villas near Paddington. The office also moved and overlooked the Thames near Charing Cross at 8 Adelphi Terrace. Although Hardy moved back to Bockhampton in 1867 following ill health and depression he returned to London to work for T Roger Smith in March 1872 – two years before his marriage to Emma Gifford on 17 September 1874. He lived during this time at 4 Celbridge Place while he courted his future wife and the couple eventually set up home in Surbiton on Hook Road. Once Hardy's reputation began to spread they moved to the more salubrious address of 18 Newton Road, Westbourne Grove, London. The newlyweds then moved south and lived in Swanage for a time before returning to the capital in March 1878 where they found a home a 1 Arundel Terrace in Tooting. While Hardy suffered illness, he and his wife decided that a permanent residence in London would not benefit either Hardy's health or their marriage. However, the Hardys continued to rent a house or flat in London each year between April and July including 16 Pelham Crescent, in South Kensington, SW7, which they rented on two separate occasions.

During his early adult years, while working for Gerald Crickmay, Hardy lived at 3 Wooperton Street in Weymouth before he and Emma Hardy lived at Riverside Villa in Sturminster Newton early on in their marriage following their time in

Surbiton. The couple lived in the Villa between 1876 and 1878 overlooking the Sour River and in March 1997, the house received a blue plaque to commemorate the time that the Hardys made Riverside Villa their home. But it was at the house he designed, Max Gate, where Hardy enjoyed the happiest days of his life. The redbrick residence can be found just south of Dorchester. He remained here for 43 years until his death at the grand age of 88.

BELOW The coffin of Thomas Hardy leaves his home at Max Gate

CLASSIC LITERATURE

Chapter 2

The Novels

The Poor Man And The Lady (1867, unpublished)

Written in 1867, *The Poor Man And The Lady* was Hardy's first novel. Having been rejected by a number of publishers, large sections of the book were destroyed, but years later the author had thought to revive the manuscript and rewrite from memory the missing prose. This idea never reached fruition.

Turned down by Macmillan but accepted for publication by Chapman and Hall, the publisher's reader, renowned novelist, George Meredith, begged Hardy not to go through with publication. He strongly believed that the book's satire of the upper classes and social messages that Hardy was trying to get across would lead to a violent attack by critics and public alike which would undoubtedly crush the author's career before it had ever got off the ground. Instead, Meredith suggested that Hardy concentrate his efforts on a purely artistic endeavour with a more complicated plot. The result was *Desperate Remedies*, published in 1871.

However, Hardy did use some of the themes in later work, especially in the poem *The Poor Man And The Lady* and in the short novel *An Indiscretion In The*

Life Of An Heiress (1878). The remains of the original manuscript were either lost
or destroyed by the writer during his final years.

CLASSIC LITERATURE

Under The Greenwood Tree (1872)

Hardy chose his own family home on which to base Tranter Dewy's house in the novel and St Michael's church in Stinsford for the Mellstock quire's formal gatherings. It was here that Fancy Day first sat at the new arrival – the organ. St George's statue in Weymouth was the setting for part of Chapter 3 while the Schoolhouse in Lower Bockhampton (where Hardy himself was briefly a pupil) was used to depict where Fancy Day taught the village children.

CLASSIC LITERATURE

Published anonymously in 1872, *Under The Greenwood Tree* concerns the activities of a group of church musicians. Dick Dewy, one of the group, becomes romantically involved with Fancy Day, the new school mistress and love triumphs, despite the fact that Fancy has a secret. She marries keeping her secret and the novel concentrates on the undertones of a happy marriage that is marred by deception. The church choir (quire) are ousted in favour of that new Victorian invention – the organ – meanwhile and Fancy's secret the fact that she was also courting the village rector Parson Maybold is kept under wraps. The critique of *The Poor Man And The* Lady by Macmillan's reader, John Morley, indicated that he thought the country scenes were the best thing in the book. Hardy took this on board and planned that *Under The*

Greenwood Tree would be "a short and quite rustic story" which would exploit what his critics said was his forte. Hardy used his experience of celebrating Christmas at a party with neighbours as the basis for his story and took the scenes he'd already written from his first unpublished manuscript that hadn't already been rewritten for *Desperate Remedies*.

Hardy called the new book *The Mellstock Quire* but changed the title to *Under The Greenwood Tree* whereupon Tinsley published the novel and paid the author £30 for the copyright. When a Tauchnitz edition was printed, the author received a further £10. The novel was a success for Tinsley who would ask for £300 from Hardy when the author wanted to buy back the copyright some years later. A pirate edition

CLASSIC LITERATURE

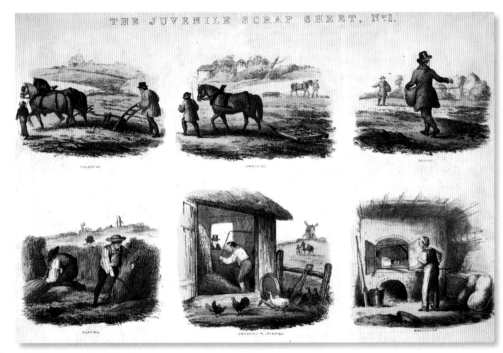

ABOVE & RIGHT
Tasks during Hardy's time

even appeared in the US a year after the initial publication and reviews were good. The novel brought the author to the attention of the renowned Leslie Stephen who literally launched Hardy's career when he asked him to contribute to *The Cornhill*. The character of Dick Dewy is "a little above himself" and he and Fancy Day are not written as such interesting characters as the Mellstock quire "rustics". Hardy chooses instead to give the interest to characters such as Dewy's father, the village

"tranter" or carrier Robert Penny, the shoemaker and Leaf, the simpleton as well as Geoffrey Day, the gamekeeper and Fancy's father. The conversations that abound between these and other "rustic" characters delighted the critics and readership alike. What Hardy was actually trying to do was show the middle classes that country people were not the inarticulate yokels they thought they were.

Interestingly, the book depicts many of Hardy's own childhood memories of country life, however, there are no children in the plot. But, just as the Hardy family lived by the seasons, the book too, is divided into four sections with each having its own tranquil timelessness. The book is earthy and real, yet lacks the tragedies of all his other novels. It is obvious in the novel that Hardy liked and respected women – perhaps more so than any other 19th century novelist – as the character of Fancy Day suggests. She and Dick Dewy are brought up in a rural reality, although Fancy Day has been educated to a higher standard than her suitor. She accepts the rector's proposal because he has great praise for her and this she is flattered by even though she is already engaged to Dewy. The rector would have been a tempting proposition for the young school teacher. Marriage to a clergyman would have propelled her social status, but she remains true to her heart and marries the lowlier Dewy. Hardy kept alive the importance of the country and a rural way of life. When he was born in 1840 agriculture was the most important industry in England. By the early 1900s the agricultural workforce had declined to less than half, but in *Under The Greenwood Tree* he sets the book at around the time he was born. He makes little mention of the fight that rural communities would have to endure to try and overcome the rural demise. In fact, the most difficult modernisation occurs for the quire in the arrival of the organ (harmonium) when bass-viols and other instruments are replaced by a larger, louder, single instrument, marking the change in the rural landscape. And the secret? It remained a secret, at least it did from Dick Dewy.

Far From The Madding Crowd (1874)

Waterston House was the building that Bathsheba Everdene would inherit from her uncle in the novel and Tithe Barn, at Cerne Abbas, was chosen for Gabriel Oak's sheep shearing. Lulworth Cove was the setting the author chose for Sergeant Troy's ill-fated swim while Puddletown church is where Fanny Robin was buried.

ABOVE Sergeant Troy swam from Lulworth Cove

The novel, *Far From The Madding Crowd*, was the first published work to put Hardy permanently on the literary map. It brought him widespread critical acclaim through its serialisation in *The Cornhill*, published by Virginia Woolf's father, Leslie Stephen. Early critics compared Hardy to writers such as George Eliot and he

became an important and recognised voice in English fiction. As with all his novels, Hardy was interested in local dialects and brought them to his writing and he was keen to portray the loss of rural life, which he saw as endangered. In this novel, as in his others, he was creating a picture for future generations to observe and be made aware of.

Bathsheba Everdene, a beautiful young woman without an amassed fortune, meets a young farmer during one evening. Bathsheba saves Gabriel Oak's life which convinces the farmer to ask the heroine to marry him. However, as she is not in love with the young man, Bathsheba declines his offer. The heroine then inherits her uncle's prosperous farm and moves away to Weatherbury. Meanwhile, Oak suffers great misfortune and loses his sheep and as a result is forced to give up his farming life. He is in need of work and his travels take him to Weatherbury. He manages to save a local farm from a fire and asks the farm's mistress (Bathsheba) if she has need of a shepherd. Oak is hired and Bathsheba sets about learning to manage her farm whereupon she becomes acquainted with her neighbour William Boldwood, a reserved and "wooden" man who becomes her suitor when on a whim she sends him a valentine which reads: "Marry Me". Boldwood then becomes obsessed with the young woman running the farm next door. However, because she does not love her rich and handsome neighbour, Bathsheba refuses him, but then agrees to reconsider her decision.

But, that same night, Bathsheba meets Sergeant Francis (Frank) Troy who falls in love with her. However, he has recently had a relationship with a local orphaned girl, Fanny Robin, who is now pregnant with the soldier's baby.

ABOVE A still from the film, *Far From The Madding Crowd* directed by John Schlesinger, 1967

Although Troy almost married Fanny Robin, he is now infatuated with Bathsheba and this in turn enrages William Boldwood, who has had his fair share of women who wanted to marry him. Bathsheba travels to Bath to warn her young suitor of her neighbour's fury, but while there, is convinced to

CLASSIC LITERATURE

marry Troy. Gabriel Oak, meanwhile, has been a constant friend and support to his mistress and does not approve of the marriage.

Just weeks after marrying Bathsheba, Troy meets with Fanny, who by now is sick and weak. She dies in childbirth and eventually Bathsheba discovers that Troy was the baby's father. For his part, Troy is fraught with shame over what has happened to Fanny and grief stricken at her death. He runs away and there are rumours that he has drowned. Now that Troy is conveniently gone, Boldwood once again begins his pursuit of Bathsheba. However, Troy spots her at a local fair and decides that he wishes to return to his wife.

At Christmas, Boldwood asks Bathsheba once again to marry him and this time she agrees. Plans are dashed though when Troy arrives and makes claim to his wife. The tragedy is worsened when Boldwood shoots Troy dead and is then sentenced to death, although this is later changed to life in prison. After a few months, Gabriel Oak, who is by now a prosperous bailiff, and Bathsheba are married.

The character of Gabriel Oak is marked as a quiet observer throughout much of the book who has humble and honest ways. He is, however, in tune with others and knows just when to step in to help with a catastrophe while the beautiful Bathsheba is rash, vain and impulsive. Troy, is the story's antagonist and similar to Bathsheba, however, he is capable of love and is unable to forgive himself when his former love dies with their child in her arms. Boldwood is cold and distant until he develops feelings for the protagonist. From this point on he becomes irrational and obsessive while the character of Fanny Robin is the foil to Bathsheba and is used to show the fate of women who are abandoned and uncared for in society. It was in *Far From The Madding Crowd* that Hardy's Wessex was first developed to resemble its more final form that was adopted for the later novels which Hardy was keen to utilise as a territorial definition for his "local" works.

The Return Of The Native (1878)

The flora and fauna of Puddletown Heath was the main setting for the novel. Renamed Egdon Heath, the location backs almost right down to the cottage where Hardy was born and comprises rolling countryside which is characterised by highly acidic soil, good for bracken and gorse. Today, the heath is heavily forested, although during Hardy's time it was fairly open land. The heath was originally covered in wild ponies, known as heath-croppers, and it was two of these wild animals that the novelist used to pull the wagon of Diggory Venn, one of the book's chief characters. Currently, heath-croppers are only found in small

ABOVE The type of scenery that inspired Hardy

numbers on Exmoor or in the New Forest in Hampshire. Shadwater Weir was the setting that Hardy chose as the setting for the climax of the book, where two major characters meet their death by drowning.

Thomasin Yeobright is in the back of Diggory Venn's wagon having found her marriage to Damon Wildeve delayed by an error found on the marriage certificate. Wildeve orchestrated the error which resulted in the collapse of his fiancée as he is infatuated with another woman, Eustacia Vye. To some extent, the reason for the deception is to make Eustacia jealous that he might be about to marry someone else. Meanwhile, Diggory Venn is in love with Thomasin and when he learns of the romance between Wildeve and Eustacia he feels vindicated in interfering on Thomasin's behalf (something he will continue to do throughout the novel). However, the reddleman's attempts to persuade Eustacia to allow Wildeve to marry Thomasin prove fruitless.

In order to escape the confused tangled web of love, Eustacia promises herself that she will fall in love with Thomasin's cousin Clym Yeobright before she has even met him. He is the son of Mrs Yeobright, Thomasin's aunt and legal guardian. So determined is Eustacia that she will leave the place she hates that she calls off her romance with Damon Wildeve who in turn feels he has little choice but to marry Thomasin.

Chance meetings and Eustacia's determination bring her and Clym Yeobright together and they begin a courtship which results in marriage despite the objections of Yeobright's mother. When Wildeve is told of the subsequent marriage of his former love his feelings are reawakened for Eustacia despite his own recent nuptials and the birth of his and Thomasin's daughter, Eustacia.

Having married someone his mother does not approve of, Clym finds himself distanced from his mother but also notices that he and his new wife are fairly distant too and he rejects her plans of a move to Paris. He wants to start a school in his native country. Meanwhile, Wildeve inherits a substantial fortune and he and an unhappy Eustacia begin to spend more time together both in public and at her home (while her husband is asleep). During this particular visit, Mrs Yeobright calls on the newlyweds looking for reconciliation. Eustacia panics and refuses to let her mother-in-law in which sees the older woman leaving her son's residence heartbroken. Her walk home is too much and she succumbs to the heat whereupon she is bitten by a snake and dies alone.

ABOVE *The Return of the Native,* audio CD

Clym Yeobright blames himself for his mother's death and he separates from his wife when he learns the truth about her visit to the house that day. Eustacia plans an escape aided by Wildeve who intends to leave with her. The night chosen for their elopement is stormy and on her way to meet her former love she is drowned. Wildeve who sees what's happening and tries to save Eustacia is also drowned and Diggory Venn manages to save Clym from the same plight through his determined heroics. Eventually Thomasin and Diggory are married and Clym who by now is a shadow of his former self becomes a preacher who is not taken particularly seriously by the local congregations he encounters.

CLASSIC LITERATURE

Clym Yeobright is the "native" of the novel's title and he returns to his home on Egdon Heath. As a diamond merchant in Paris he finds that it is not material wealth he's seeking which conflicts strongly with his wife's desire to move there in an effort to escape the heath which she loathes. Having studied for many hours, his degenerative eye condition worsens and perhaps his physical demise only enhances his emotional crisis as he blames himself for both the deaths of his mother and wife. In complete contrast to Clym, Damon Wildeve is more interested in possession than love while his wife, Thomasin, who does care for him, makes the cruel decision to name their child Eustacia to haunt her former rival.

Although Hardy was formally conventional in his approach with this novel which adheres closely to the Victorian style, the author is also rather keen to insert much doubt and ambiguity into the story and he uses the heath cleverly as a place which brings about endless unreliability. The ending is also bleak – much like the heath in many parts of the book – particularly in terms of how the novelist views human nature. The reason that Diggory and Thomasin have a contented marriage at the end of the novel was because Hardy was obliged to provide a "happy" ending for the Victorian readership.

The novel was considered to have themes of a controversial nature during the late 1800s with its open acknowledgement of illicit sexual relationships and reviews, although mixed, were fairly positive. It would become one of Hardy's most popular novels during the 20th century with its sexual politics, thwarted desire and the conflicting demands of nature and society.

Although several stage adaptations of the book have occurred the only film version was made as a television movie in 1994. Starring Catherine Zeta Jones as Eustacia Vye and Clive Owen as Damon Wildeve the location chosen for the filming was Exmoor. Another television adaptation was expected sometime in 2008.

The Mayor Of Casterbridge (1886)

The King's Arms Hotel in Dorchester is the setting for the King's Arms in the town of Casterbridge. With its spacious bow window stretching out over the street it is here that Susan Henchard and her daughter observe the new Mayor while a building that is now a prominent high street bank is used for the Mayor's house. The Roman amphitheatre, The Maumbry Rings, is the setting for the first secret reunion between Henchard and Susan while Grey's Bridge is where Henchard comes to meditate his melancholic mood.

It was *The Mayor Of Casterbridge*, along with *The Woodlanders*, *Tess Of The d'Urbervilles* and *Jude The Obscure* that capped Hardy's career in fiction as far as many of his critics were concerned. Hardy was known to have been sensitive to what others thought of his work and the critique by

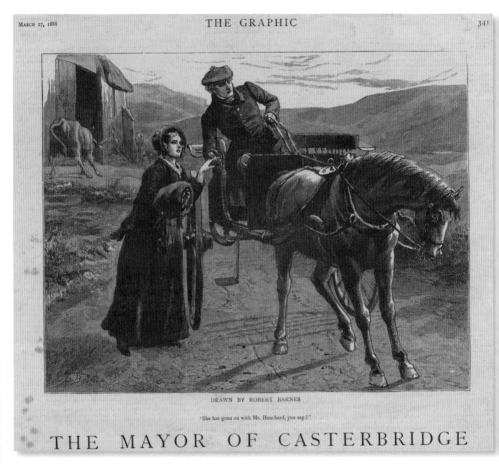

DRAWN BY ROBERT BARNES

'She has gone on with Mr. Henchard, you say?'

THE MAYOR OF CASTERBRIDGE

Havelock Ellis in the April 1883 edition of the *Westminster Review* of Hardy's novels up to that date seems to have struck a chord. The essay was decidedly positive about the author's work and offered evaluations that changed the way in which Hardy would portray his characters. This particular novel is the first that does not use a protagonist or centre around a profession (such as architecture) that the author needs to have some knowledge of while he was keen to advance from a plot that was driven by love. So, spurred on by the need for development and change, Hardy turned Michael Henchard into one of the most remarkable and dominant of all his characters against a social and historical backdrop.

The novel mainly charts the course of Michael Henchard's character with minor characters brought in around him, however, the book continues with Hardy's campaign to chronicle the dramatic and life-changing events that were taking place in turning a rural agricultural community into a bustling modern city. As he did later in both *Tess* and *Jude*, the author is also striving to explore the effects of cultural and economic developments and the rise of urbanisation and industrialisation.

Travelling with his wife, Susan, Michael Henchard is looking for employment as a hay-trusser. Having stopped for a rest, Henchard gets drunk and in an auction that begins as a joke and ends seriously he sells his wife and their baby daughter for five guineas to a sailor by the name of Newson. He bitterly regrets his actions the following

CLASSIC LITERATURE

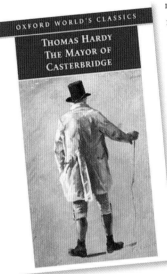

ABOVE The Mayor of Casterbridge, novel

morning but is unable to find his family. He swears on oath in a nearby church that he will not touch alcohol for 21 years (the same number of years as his age). Eighteen years later, Newson dies and Susan and Elizabeth-Jane decide to seek out Michael Henchard.

Elizabeth-Jane believes Henchard to be a long-lost relative and upon arriving in Casterbridge, mother and daughter learn that he is now the town mayor. The formerly married couple meet in secret and so not to cause their daughter any pain or confusion agree to court and marry as if they had only just met. In the meantime, Henchard has employed Donald Farfrae as the new manager of his corn business and Elizabeth-Jane becomes intrigued by the young Scot. Farfrae outwits Henchard at every turn and makes the older man so frustrated that he asks him to leave the company and to stop courting his daughter. Soon after marriage to Henchard, Susan falls ill and dies and it is then that he finds out that Elizabeth-Jane is not his daughter after all, she is Newson's. Henchard's daughter, Elizabeth-Jane died as a young child and when Susan and Newson had a daughter she took her late half-sister's name. He becomes very cold towards his only "daughter". Confused by events, Elizabeth-Jane leaves her "father's" house and moves in with Lucetta Templeman, a lady with whom Henchard was romantically involved during Susan's 18-year absence. Lucetta now wants to marry Henchard. In the meantime, Farfrae visits Miss Templeman's home in order to call on Elizabeth-Jane. He and Lucetta find they are taken with each other, however, and are eventually married.

Because of her marriage to Farfrae, Lucetta asks Henchard to return all the letters she sent him. He complies, however, the messenger, a man by the name of Jopp stops at the inn on his journey and he is convinced to open some letters where they are read aloud. A humiliating parade is then held, while Farfrae is away on business, and Lucetta on seeing the spectacle faints. The events make her very ill and she dies soon afterward. But, while Henchard has come to hate Farfrae, he has changed his mind about Elizabeth-Jane and becomes incredibly closer to her.

A further twist in the tale takes place when Newson, who was not actually dead after all, arrives at Henchard's house and asks after his daughter. Henchard, in bitterness, tells the man Elizabeth-Jane is dead and Newson leaves heartbroken.

ABOVE Alan Bates who played the part of Henchard

Elizabeth-Jane remains with Henchard and begins to spend more time with Farfrae and then Newson arrives back in town. Henchard, on hearing this news, decides to leave town and Newson and his daughter are reunited. A wedding is planned between Elizabeth-Jane and Farfrae. The night of the wedding Henchard returns to ask Elizabeth-Jane for forgiveness. She snubs him and Henchard leaves town telling her he will not return. However, the young woman regrets her decision and sets off

CLASSIC LITERATURE

ABOVE Ciarin Hinds who played the role of Henchard

with Farfrae to find Henchard. They arrive to find he has died alone in the countryside where his last dying wish was to be forgotten.

This tragic tale was adapted twice as a mini-series, first in 1978 starring Alan Bates as Henchard and then again in 2003 with Ciaran Hinds in the lead role. The book was also adapted as an opera by Peter Tranchell the renowned British composer.

The Woodlanders (1887)

This novel was reportedly Hardy's favourite novel, despite it being less well known than the four prolific titles: *The Mayor Of Casterbridge, Tess Of The d'Urbervilles, Jude The Obscure* and *The Return Of The Native*.

Grace Melbury, the educated daughter of timber merchant, George Melbury, is feeling isolated and alienated from her childhood home and friends since having been away at school. She returns home to Little Hintock where her future has already been decided. Grace is to marry Giles Winterborne, an employee at her father's timber yard. He, for his part, has been in love with Grace for a number of years. The arranged marriage was George Melbury's idea to make up for an injustice that Giles's father suffered some time before. Although Grace was previously happy about the idea of marrying the man she loves, on her return, her dissatisfaction with the arrangement is steadily growing. With going away to school, Grace has been fortunate and has seen a great deal more than she feels Little Hintock has

to offer her. Her father, meanwhile, is greatly torn between the promise he made to Giles's father and his feelings that now Grace has had a good education perhaps she deserves more than to end up back where she started with Giles who has little to offer her.

The arrival in the village of Edred Fitzpiers, an ambitious young doctor, causes quite a stir among the village's young women and when Grace meets him for the first time she is filled with the beginnings of a sense of ambition. However, Grace

CLASSIC LITERATURE

is not the only villager to fall for the young doctor. The air of mystery surrounding Edred Fitzpiers only makes him more enticing.

To make matters more complicated, Giles is evicted from his home by Mrs Charmond, a lady who lives alone in Hintock House. To further create suspense,

BELOW Felicity Kendal who played the part of Grace Melbury

Marty South, a young penniless villager, is madly in love with Giles and begins a pursuit of the man she wants to spend her life with. With dwindling finances, George Melbury slowly becomes convinced that Giles is not a suitable match for his daughter, however, both Grace's promised love and the young doctor begin to court her. The choice over which man to marry leaves Grace with a difficult decision. What doesn't help is all the rumours she hears about one of her suitor's indiscretions.

The Woodlanders comprises social obligation and self-discovery and Grace very definitely sets out on a journey to discover what is important in life. Hardy cleverly constructs a plot which shows clearly how restricting and debilitating social structures were and the woodland which surrounds the isolated village is given a particularly oppressive feel. Grace eventually, having become somewhat hesitant and prone to changing her mind decides to marry Fitzpiers, however, her true love is for Giles. A little while after the marriage it transpires that Fitzpiers is having an affair with Mrs Charmond and begins to become very cold towards his wife. He finally deserts Grace one night after accidentally revealing his true nature to his father-in-law.

George Melbury's attempts to get his daughter a divorce from her errant husband prove to be in vain while Fitzpiers quarrels with Mrs Charmond and decides to return to Little Hintock in order to try a reconciliation with his wife. But Grace is having none of it and flees to Giles and asks for help. He meanwhile is convalescing from a dangerous illness, but still allows Grace to stay in his hut – while he gallantly sleeps outside. The night is stormy and Giles later dies. Grace allows herself to be won back, if just temporarily, by a repentant husband, and no one is there to mourn Giles, except Marty South, the only one who loved him unconditionally right from the beginning.

There have been two adaptations of the novel, one by the BBC in 1970 starring Felicity Kendal and a 1997 film version which starred Rufus Sewell as Giles Winterbourne, Emily Woof as Grace Melbury and Jodhi May as Marty South.

CLASSIC LITERATURE

Wessex Tales (a collection of short stories, 1888)

The tales are all set in a time before Hardy's birth and grounded firmly in life in rural Dorset and folklore before the mid-1800s. Published in 1888, *Wessex Tales* includes titles such as The Melancholy Hussar Of The German Legion, The Withered Arm, The Distracted Preacher, The Three Strangers, Fellow Townsmen and A Tradition Of Eighteen Hundred And Four. In these tales, Hardy creates a fictional world to represent the hierarchy of shepherds, artisans and craftspeople,

ABOVE Rural life that Hardy wrote so fondly about

quite unlike the usual aristocratic literature that the Victorian era was used to. In order to ensure the stories were factually correct, Hardy poured over old newspapers and parish records. He also spoke with people who would be able to give him insight into the past. He uses the pastoral voice to portray each tale thereby giving nature a voice through his writing. It was common for 19th century poets to write in this way.

LEFT The type of craftsmen depicted in his writings

CLASSIC LITERATURE

" It was not till about three o'clock that Tess raised her eyes and gave a momentary glance round. She felt but little surprise at seeing that Alec D'Urberville had come back, and was standing under the hedge by the gate."

"TESS OF THE D'URBERVILLES"

By THOMAS HARDY,

AUTHOR OF "FAR FROM THE MADDING CROWD," "THE MAYOR OF CASTERBRIDGE," &c., &c.

ILLUSTRATED BY PROFESSOR HUBERT HERKOMER, R.A., AND HIS PUPILS, MESSRS. WEHRSCHMIDT, JOHNSON, AND SYDALL

Tess Of The d'Urbervilles (1891)

Woolbridge Manor is often referred to as Wellbridge House, where Angel Clare and Tess retreated after their wedding, while the Vale of Blackmoor was the setting for much of the novel. It was this novel that was to secure Hardy's financial future, despite the fact it received a fair amount of criticism for the author's openly sympathetic attitude to a "fallen" woman. Here he demonstrates his deep understanding and empathy with the lower classes and the book courted controversy for its frank portrayal of the sexual hypocrisy of English society. Writing at a time of slow change between tradition and innovation, "new" money was elevating businessmen and entrepreneurs up into the ranks of the social elite while those with "old" money – the higher echelons of English society – were beginning to fade.

This particular novel outlines the change when a chance meeting between Tess's father, Durbeyfield, and a stranger means the old man loses himself in a fantasy of belong to aristocracy and the d'Urberville family. The novel goes to great lengths to portray this kind of aristocratic family not only as undesirable but quite simply meaningless. This view, of course, appalled the status-conscious readership and Hardy was increasingly frustrated by the controversy which surrounded the novel (this would further be compounded when *Jude The Obscure* was published four years later.

Walking home after a chance encounter with a stranger, John Durbeyfield, a poor peddler, is astonished to discover that he is the descendant of the d'Urbervilles. Tess is enjoying the May Day celebrations with other girls from the village. While dancing with her friends, Tess exchanges glances with a young man. He later turns out to be Angel Clare, the son of a rector and esteemed family of clergymen.

LEFT Innocent Tess looks up from her work

CLASSIC LITERATURE

RIGHT Natassja Kinski, in Roman Polanski's film *Tess*

Meanwhile, she is sent to the d'Urberville family home, where the Durbeyfields hope that Tess will make her fortune under the guidance of Mrs d'Urberville. However, although the older woman cares deeply for her animals she views Tess as little more than an impoverished girl and does not treat her, or her maid Elizabeth and even her son Alec particularly well. It turns out that Mrs d'Urberville is not related to Tess in fact and that her late husband, Simon Stokes simply changed his name to d'Urberville on his retirement. But Tess is unaware of this fact and blaming herself for an accident involving the family's horse she feels she has no choice but to accept a job tending fowls on the estate.

For several months Tess is confined to caring for the birds and resists all attempts by Alec d'Urberville to seduce her. After a local fair, however, Alex takes advantage of Tess and she finds herself pregnant. Returning home to give birth to her child, Sorrow. The baby boy dies soon after he is born and is unable to be buried in consecrated ground due to his mother's unmarried status. After a miserable year, Tess finally takes a job as a milkmaid at Talbothays Dairy where she finds contentment and happiness among the other workers. She establishes good friendships with other milkmaids Izz, Retty and Marian who remain lifelong friends even though they themselves all fall in love with Angel Clare who is also at the dairy learning about farming. He has doubts about his faith and has opted to become a farmer rather than follow his father and brothers into the clergy.

He and Tess slowly fall in love and she eventually accepts his proposal of marriage. However, she feels that Angel should know the truth about her past and writes a note which she slips under his door one night. Unfortunately, the note is slipped under the carpet and the young groom-to-be never sees it. After their wedding the young couple discuss their past histories and Angel confesses his affair with an older woman in London. Tess immediately forgives him, but Angel is completely unable to reconcile himself with her own story about Alec and the death

CLASSIC LITERATURE

of her son. He gives Tess money and sets off for Brazil where he aims to establish his own farm. He tells Tess that he will also try to accept her past but that she should not try to find him until he comes back for her.

Tess then has a particularly difficult time where she struggles to find work and eventually when she does it is on an unpleasant farm. She then sets off to see Angel's family but overhears his brothers discussing his "poor marriage" and thinks better of it. Later, she hears a wandering preacher speak to a crowd and is surprised to discover that the preacher is none other than Alec d'Urberville – who was converted to Christianity by Angel's father. Each is shaken by the encounter and Alec begs Tess not to tempt him again. However, he then begs her to marry him when he decides abruptly to abandon religion. Tess returns home when her younger sister Liza-Lu informs her of her mother's impending death. But, Joan Durbeyfield makes a full recovery, however, John Durbeyfield dies shortly after and the family is evicted from their home. Alec offers his help, but Tess refuses, knowing that it would only obligate her to him.

Meanwhile, Angel Clare has decided to forgive his wife and he leaves Brazil desperate to find her. He finds Mrs Durbeyfield who advises him that Tess is living in a village called Sandbourne. He discovers her in an expensive boarding house – where she is living with Alec d'Urberville. However, overcome with years of pent up emotion, Tess stabs Alec to death and flees to find a heartbroken Angel. The landlady discovers Alec's body and raises the alarm and by this time, Angel has agreed to help Tess although he is stunned that she actually killed Alec.

The couple hide in an empty mansion for a few days and then set off further on their travels. They rest at Stonehenge, but the police are trailing them and Tess is arrested and sent to jail. Tess is executed and the black flag raised above the building signals to Angel and Liza-Lu that Tess is gone. The two hold hands and walk silently away.

The unfair way in which some lives turn out is explored fully in this novel. Despite the fact that the Durbeyfields are of noble blood, the fact almost remains irrelevant to all other characters in the novel. Mrs Clare, who later comes to appreciate Tess is at first snobbish and disappointed that her son has chosen an impoverished young woman as his wife. Mrs d'Urberville treats her as no more than a servant and it is clear throughout that money means more than heritage. Even

CLASSIC LITERATURE

though Angel Clare comes from an aristocratic background he chooses to work alongside farm labourers and Alec d'Urberville is purely among the social elite because his father bought an ancient family name and had money.

There is great confusion in the novel about what class actually is and the three main characters all strike off in different directions from the class that they were born into. Hardy also makes no bones about the way in which men of the era were able to dominate and control women. This was greatly offensive to the majority of the readership who accepted that women were inferior to men. Obviously, Alec's rape of Tess is the most outrageous example of this, however, even Angel Clare seems to have a mental picture of what Tess should be like and rejects her once he is given the real facts about the person that she has become due to the circumstances she suffered.

The novel is disturbing and exciting and completely fresh compared to other novels of its time. It is little wonder that with such insight Hardy managed to evoke such a reaction. Some critics believe that *Tess Of The d'Urbervilles* is highly overrated, however, Hardy's brave, realistic and stoic attempt to show the changing face of society and the limits, restrictions and unjust way in which the lower classes, and women particularly, were treated remains as important today as it did at the turn of the 20th century. Despite the fact that class does not exist now as it did, there are still elements of society that believe themselves superior to others while abusive men are still very much a part of everyday life.

Jude The Obscure *(1895)*

Despite the critical acclaim as an author that Hardy had already received, when *Jude The Obscure* was published in 1895 he gave up writing novels altogether because of the enormous controversy that surrounded the book. The way in which the author focused on the institution of marriage was particularly offensive to the sensitivities of society at the time. Even Hardy's own wife, Emma Gifford Hardy, was convinced that the public would see the book as an autobiographical account of the couple's own marriage which upset her greatly. The book became so offensive in some quarters that the Bishop of Exeter is reported to have burnt a copy.

The novel was renamed *Jude The Obscene* by at least one reviewer and many other reviews were particularly harsh. The novel also openly explores sexuality, especially of the main characters, Jude and his love, Sue. It was socially unacceptable at the time and the plot was substantially altered for the novel's serialisation which was published under the name *The Simpletons* and later as *Hearts Insurgent* in the European and US editions of *Harper's New Monthly* magazine between the end of 1894 and November 1895. This was insisted upon by the publishers for moral reasons and Hardy felt totally incensed by the strong reaction the "true" version evoked when it was published in full.

Oxford was renamed Christminster for the novel, while the Martyres' Cross, a monument to Cranmer, Latimer and Ridley, the Protestant martyrs was the spot chosen in the city where Jude asks Sue to meet him for the first time.

ABOVE Thomas Hardy *Jude The Obscure*, Novel

CLASSIC LITERATURE

LEFT Stonemason's at work in Oxford in Hardy's day

The elaborate plot centres around the character of Jude Fawley, who was orphaned and brought up by his working class aunt. However, he dreams of becoming a scholar at Christminster but finds that his background leads him into a career as a stonemason instead. His inspiration for scholarly success came from Richard Phillotson, the schoolmaster who left for the city when Jude was still a child. As Jude reaches maturity he falls in love with Arabella, but is tricked into marrying her which confines him to a life of staying in the village where he was brought up. The marriage goes sour and Arabella travels to Australia leaving Jude free to follow his ambition of leaving for Christminster where his attempts to enrol at university are met with little enthusiasm.

While in Christminster, Jude meets his cousin Sue Bridehead and promises himself not to fall in love although he does arrange for her to work with Richard Phillotson so that she can remain in the city. He is extremely disappointed when he learns that Sue is to marry Phillotson and, after the wedding takes place, he learns further that his cousin is deeply unhappy with her situation. She leaves her husband to set up home with Jude and both couples divorce. However, Sue does not want to remarry and Jude is surprised to learn that he and Arabella have a son whom she asks Jude to care for. The couple have two children of their own and bring up Jude and Arabella's young son as their own. Jude becomes ill and when he recovers, the family, who have been living back in his childhood village decide to return to Christminster. But here they have trouble finding lodgings because of their unmarried status.

CLASSIC LITERATURE

Eventually, Jude is forced to stay at a nearby inn, away from Sue and the children. One fateful day, Sue, having had breakfast with Jude in his room, returns with him to her lodgings to find that Jude's son has hung both himself and the other two children. The little boy had decided that Jude and Sue would be better off without them. Sue, who has become increasingly religious as the story unravels, feels that the deaths of the children is God's way of punishing her and she reluctantly returns to Phillotson. Meanwhile, Jude is once again tricked into living with Arabella and he dies soon after visiting Sue one last time during torrential weather.

The subtle details and the ensuing accidents lead to the ruin of both Jude and Sue. Hardy condemns many elements of life in the novel including how even when free to fulfil dreams and ambitions, social class will limit how far those dreams and ambitions can be obtained. He also questions religion in terms of how when faced with ruin there is no heavenly redemption while also exploring the fact that if life is lived in integrity (through passion) society will merely see that type of relationship as scandalous. He focuses on deep loneliness and sexuality and cleverly manipulates the downfall of the characters, almost sadistically. It is not difficult to see how these elements would have greatly offended a moralistic and tradition society, however, what the author did express was critically important and poignant.

Although outrageous to many, the infanticide was crucially the turning point for the central characters. It persuaded a woman, who had barely wanted any sexual relations at all, that she was being punished for abandoning her obligations to society and her husband. The characters were then condemned to miserable lives, and in Jude's case, death, much in the same way they had been when trying to live together and bring up children out of wedlock. The book was hard-hitting and passionate in its beliefs and the story is still as shocking (in terms of aspects of the plot) to read today as it would have been in 1895.

Other notable titles

So many of Hardy's novels are extremely important to our understanding of his beliefs and thoughts as a writer. Hardy, like Jane Austen, did not particularly belong to one era or another. Writing around the turn of the 19th and 20th centuries he was often described as Victorian, because of the language he used and the terminology he associated with his work, however, he was also on the cusp of a

BELOW The Napoleonic War inspired the *Trumpet Major*

CLASSIC LITERATURE

RIGHT The Dorset
Coast

great change – even if it was slow in progressing – and was consumed with modern thinking, which was so evident in his novels.

Written in 1873, *A Pair Of Blue Eyes* was based around much of his four-year courtship with Emma Gifford, prior to their wedding in 1874. It was the first published work to have Hardy's name on it and the novel centres around the character of Elfride Swancourt, a young woman who is caught up in a battle between her heart, her mind and society's expectations of her. This was not unlike that of Hardy's own wife whose family greatly disapproved of their relationship. Emma Gifford was, in fact, from a higher class then her husband and using the character of Stephen Smith, a social inferior, but ambitious young man to represent the rural, more rustic way of life and Henry Knight, a respectable, established older man to draw on the expectation of London society, Hardy paints parallels between the novel and his own relationship.

The Trumpet Major published in 1880 had been carefully written by Hardy who visited Chelsea Hospital on 18 June 1875 (Waterloo Day) to talk to survivors of the battle some 60 years before. He made several visits to the hospital and he also made a pilgrimage to the battlefield itself after being inspired by the Napoleonic Wars having found a scrapbook

belonging to his grandfather, who had himself been a private in the Puddletown Volunteer Light Infantry.

This novel and *The Dynasts* were inspired by the stories that Hardy was told, they fuelled his imagination and formed an important history of England that had remained untold in publications up to that point which were relayed to Hardy by his paternal grandmother over the invasion scare in Dorset. The novel's heroine, Ann Garland, is avidly pursued by three potential suitors: John Loveday, a trumpet major in a British regiment who is depicted as honest and true, the cowardly Festus Derriman and Loveday's brother Bob, a womanising merchant seaman. Set in the Napoleonic Wars, this is an unusual novel for Hardy in that all the main characters are not disgraced, admonished and abandoned and they live happily at the end of the story. The novel inspired the opera *The Trumpet Major* by Alun Hoddinott which was first performed in the UK in 1981.

Drawing inspiration from the settings of Chesil beach which connects Portland in Dorset to the mainland, Portland itself, Pennsylvania Castle, the West Wall of the castle supposedly built by King William Rufus and St George's church in Portland, *The Well Beloved* published in 1897 was Hardy's last published novel, and not *Jude The Obscure* as many people think. It was originally intended as a three-part serial publication in 1892. Like other novels given to serialisation, substantial parts of the text were changed but the full version in book form gives a great deal of information about the history of the English novel, while *The Hand Of Ethelberta* – published some years before in 1876 – is a highly comic novel which was originally serialised in Leslie Stephen's *The Cornhill*. The novel proved a fascinating read just through its sheer strange approach and Hardy once again ably portrayed the plight and conscious of its heroine, a poor ambitious woman who eventually marries into the aristocracy. But despite the author's subtitle of "A Comedy in Chapters" the novel is not a light read and there are lessons to be learned which are combined with clear and intuitive insight and delicate handling.

By contrast, *A Laodicean*, which was published in 1881, is set in a more modern age and uses devices that were considered uncharacteristic of Hardy, namely falsified telegrams and faked photographs which are used to induce the heroine, Paula Power, to marry William Dare's father, Captain De Stancy, from whose family her father bought a medieval castle which she has just inherited. Paula, however, has feelings for George Somerset whose character portrays modern society.

ABOVE The Hand of Ethelberta, novel

Eventually, after misunderstandings, Somerset and Paula are united and marry while the protagonist is left to weigh up the pros and cons between modernity and romantic medievalism. The book was dictated to Emma Gifford Hardy as the author lay bedridden, probably with typhoid fever that was further complicated by kidney stones. The final novel of note is *Two On A Tower*, published in 1882 which the author began work on in January of that year. Although less well known amongst Hardy's works, the novel is cited by critics and scholars alike as one of his more notable and remarkable achievements. It is a moving romance filled with suspense and surprising twists.

CLASSIC LITERATURE

The Poetry

Although this book predominantly covers the novels of Thomas Hardy, it would be unwise not to include the passion that fuelled the writer's life at the beginning and for the last 30 years of his life – poetry. Hardy's poetry was not published until later in his life once the novels had established his name. Much of the poetry was then published in a huge volume, and although many of the very early poems were lost, some from his first years in London survived. However, because the poems were published in substantial volumes it has been a difficult job for scholars to note any development in Hardy's style of verse. All were based on the poet's life experiences, some more heart-felt than others, and the general outpouring of grief he suffered at the loss of Emma Gifford Hardy is testament to this fact. *Neutral Tones*, a poem Hardy wrote during his London years, was particularly prolific – and highly praised – which emphasised one of the poet's major concerns: his relationships with women. Many poems were written about the experiences Hardy had when he was given the task of overseeing the removal of the old graves at St Pancras (Old Church) by his then employer Arthur Blomfield in around 1865. It was a particularly macabre assignment and is adequately pictured in his verse, including *The Levelled Churchyard*, although many suggest that Hardy was also referring (or solely referring) to the churchyard in Wimborne where he moved with his wife and which had also been restored. He wrote a great many poems connected to the grave

CLASSIC LITERATURE

but the tone in some is different where once lovers are separated by death.

When the *Wessex Poems* were published in 1898, 500 copies were printed. But there was also an American edition and both contained illustrations by the author. Four years later, 500 copies of *Poems Of The Past And Present* were published in 1902 and were followed by the dramatic, fantastical work, *The Dynasts*, Part 1, a year later. The epic trilogy depicting the Napoleonic Wars saw its print run double to 1,000 copies while Part 2, published two years later saw an initial print run of more than 1,500 copies. In 1908, Part 3 was followed by his famous poems entitled *Time's Laughingstock In 1909. Satires Of Circumstance* was published in 1914 while a corrected edition followed a year later. *Moments Of Vision* appeared two years later in 1917. In 1922 the poet published *Late Lyrics And Earlier* and *Human Shows* in 1925. The final collection of poems, *Winter Words,* from 1928 was the last official book and was published posthumously. The work was prepared under the supervision of the poet and was possibly due for publication on Hardy's 90th birthday which would have been a common occurrence at that time.

There were also a number of collected editions which were published between 1916 and 1931, some three years after Hardy's death. The first, *Selected Poems*, were published by Macmillan in 1917 and were reprinted for publication in 1917 and 1922. The Wessex Edition consisted of six

volumes of verse published between 1912 – the year of Emma Gifford Hardy's death – and 1931, which included *Human Shows* and *Winter Words* as well as all three parts of *The Dynasts*. *Collected Poems* followed in 1919 with an Anniversary Edition appearing a year later. This was in actual fact a reprint of the Wessex Edition for the American market. Between 1919 and 1920, *Mellstock Edition* comprised of seven volumes of poetry including *Satires Of Circumstance*. A Pocket Edition was then published, followed by a lavish signed edition of *The Dynasts* in 1927. The year following Hardy's death saw the publication *Chosen Poems* which he had specifically compiled himself as an expanded version of *Selected Poems*.

Other notable collections include:
The Convergence Of The Twain (1912)
Song Of The Soldiers (1914)
The Oxen (1915)
Domicilium (1916)
To Shakespeare (1916)
Yuletide In A Younger World (1927)
Christmas In The Elgin Room (1927)

Most of Hardy's poems deal with disappointment in love and life and against the indifference that mankind seemed to have for human suffering. Some poems like *The Darkling Thrush* or *An August Midnight* are actually poems about writing poetry while some poems are fairly cheerful in their approach but others are more sombre including *The Blinded Bird*. Many portrayed Hardy's love of nature (he was committed to the welfare of animals and was a member of the RSPCA).

There was some controversy over Hardy's poetry as well as his prose which has been suggested in part because the writer's place in literature has always been

controversial. He was, of course, a poetic genius who well understood his subject matter. His delicate writing and descriptive passages were well revered and his self-expression was considered second to none among his contemporaries. About 1,000 poems were published during Hardy's lifetime where two of the most well known of his war poems include *Drummer Hodge* and *In Time Of The Breaking Of Nations* which clearly show his experiences of both the Boer War and the First World War.

CLASSIC LITERATURE

Chapter 4

Hardy's Contemporaries

One of Hardy's most exciting contemporaries and no stranger to controversy himself was David Herbert Richards Lawrence, better know to the literary world as D H Lawrence (1885 – 1930). He, too, was a controversial writer whose prolific and diverse output included short stories, poems, plays, essays, travel books and novels as well as paintings, literary criticism (he was a particular critic of Hardy) and he was also concerned with the coming of the modern era and industrialisation against a backdrop of rural demise. He particularly commented on emotional health, vitality, sexuality and instinctive behaviour and associated with Hardy on many levels. But his unsettling opinions earned the writer many enemies and he would endure censorship, persecution and hardships as a result of his openness. In fact, D H Lawrence suffered even more than Hardy at the hands of an outraged public and spent the latter part of his life in voluntary exile and at the time of his untimely death was almost considered pornographic and a writer "who had wasted his talents". However, E M Forster challenged this view and wrote in an obituary that Lawrence was "the greatest imaginative novelist of our generation".

Another great writer who was aware of the work of Hardy was George Meredith, who, as already noted, advised him not to publish *Desperate Remedies* for the sake of his literary career. Meredith (1828 – 1909) began his own career, like Hardy, in a completely different profession as a trainee solicitor, however, began writing poetry

CLASSIC LITERATURE

with the encouragement of his literary friends. He helped to organise the writing of a monthly manuscript magazine and he met Edward Peacock and his beautiful sister Mary Ellen Nicholls, on whom Meredith would base many of his heroines. His first poem was published by *Chamber's Edinburgh Journal* in 1849 and it led to a small regular income from contributions in both verse and prose to various magazines. Meredith's first book of poetry was published in 1851 and four years later, he received fairly good reviews for his fantasy *The Shaving Of Shagpat*. His *Modern Love Poems* published in 1862 were largely autobiographical, something he could associate with Hardy who in the main wrote largely autobiographical works despite his protestations to the contrary. He continued to write poetry even though he stopped writing prose in 1895 (another similarity to Hardy) and his last collection of poems, *A Reading Of Life, With Other Poems*, was published eight years before his death in 1901.

William Morris (1834 – 1836) was a poet, artist, manufacturer and socialist and a contemporary of Hardy. Unlike Hardy, Morris was educated at university (Exeter College – Oxford) where he was a swift and comprehensive reader with a prodigious memory whereby he gained such knowledge in a short space of time which would help him in later life. While at Exeter College he met and befriended Edward Burne-Jones and the two men shared an intimacy that would last a lifetime.

CLASSIC LITERATURE

RIGHT Charles Dickens was a vigorous social campaigner

CLASSIC LITERATURE

Burne-Jones gave up his studies to become an artist encouraged by the renowned artist Rossetti. The artist was a strong influence on both young men and while in London Rossetti was successful in convincing Morris that he too should become a painter. By the time he and Burne-Jones were renting a studio in Holborn in 1857, Morris had already proved his prowess in imaginative literature. He found that storytelling came easily and at the same time he discovered a love for lyrical poetry which he began writing. He became one of the founders of the *Oxford And Cambridge Magazine* and contributed many pieces of prose to the publication where *The Hollow Land* was considered remarkable by critics. He married Jane Burden in 1869 and like Hardy designed his own marital home. And, just like Hardy, Morris was a man of small stature, but powerful in all things literary.

An early contemporary of Hardy was Elizabeth Gaskell (1810 – 1865) who was often referred to simply as Mrs Gaskell as was common for Victorian female writers at the time. Gaskell was a short story writer and novelist who is perhaps most well known for her biography about Charlotte Brontë, which she wrote with the help of Bronte's father, the Reverend Patrick Brontë. She was prolific in writing about the poor and also many other classes in society. Other notable works of Mrs Gaskell include her first novel, *Mary Barton* (published anonymously in 1848), *Cranford* (published a few years later in 1853), *North and South* (1854) and *Wives and Daughters* (1865). She was a friend of Charles Dickens and become extremely popular for her work especially that published by Dickens in his magazine *Household Words*.

Gaskell's friend, Charles Dickens (1812 – 1870) was also an early contemporary of Hardy. He was scarred deeply by having to remain in prison with his father (who was imprisoned for debt) until he was 12 years old. He was further damaged by his mother's insistence that he then work in a blacking factory until his father rescued him from the ordeal. Although psychologically scarred by his experiences – Dickens only ever spoke of his horrendous time at the factory to his wife and one close

CLASSIC LITERATURE

RIGHT Thackeray was famous for his satirical works

friend, John Forster – it gave him a creative energy and he became obsessed with themes of alienation and betrayal which emerged most notably in his novels, *Great Expectations* and *David Copperfield*. Dickens went on to become a freelance reporter of the legal system and a shorthand reporter at Parliamentary debates at the House of Commons before becoming a reporter for a newspaper. Following the success of *The Pickwick Papers* in the mid 1830s, he took up a career as a fulltime novelist which comprised of works of increasingly complexity. *Oliver Twist* (1837) and *Nicholas Nickleby* (1838) followed and were succeeded by other infamous titles such as *Martin Chuzzlewit* and *A Christmas Carol*. Dickens was also synonymous with London readings throughout his high profile career and was the founder of a number of magazines – which published works by the likes of Mrs Gaskell – but he was shaken by a railway accident in 1865 on his return from a holiday in Paris. In 1869 Dickens collapsed showing signs of having had a mild stroke and his final public readings took place the following year. However, he suffered another stroke on 8 June 1870 and died the next day. He was buried at Westminster Abbey and like Hardy is remembered in Poet's Corner.

William Makepeace Thackeray (1811 – 1863) was another early contemporary of Hardy and was educated at Cambridge University before he became addicted to gambling. He left without a degree and was heavily in debt and at first tried to make a living as a painter. When this proved unsuccessful he became a journalist on the French controversial publication *The Constitutional* but when the newspaper ceased publication he returned to England where he began contributing a wide variety of articles to various newspapers and journals. He began writing novels and in 1844 his first work was *Barry Lyndon* which was serialised. His most famous novel, *Vanity Fair*, was published in 1847. He remained a successful novelist up to his death in 1863.

Chapter 5

Other Works

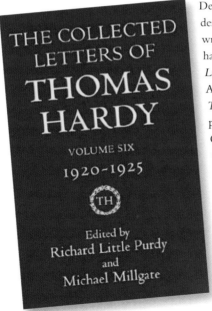

Despite many notebooks and journals being destroyed, some of Hardy's thoughts, notes, writings and musings survived and many of these have since been published. These include *The Literary Notes Of Thomas Hardy*, published by Acta Universitatis Gothoburgensis in 1974 and *The Personal Notebooks Of Thomas Hardy*, published by Macmillan in 1978 and by Columbia University Press a year later. *The Collected Letters Of Thomas Hardy* were published in seven volumes by Oxford University Press between 1978 and 1997. That same year, *Thomas Hardy's Christmas* was published by A Sutton and compiled by John Chandler, and *Thomas Hardy's Public Voice: The Essays, Speeches And Miscellaneous Prose,* edited by leading authority on the author, Michael Millgate, was published by Oxford University Press (New York, NY) in 2001.

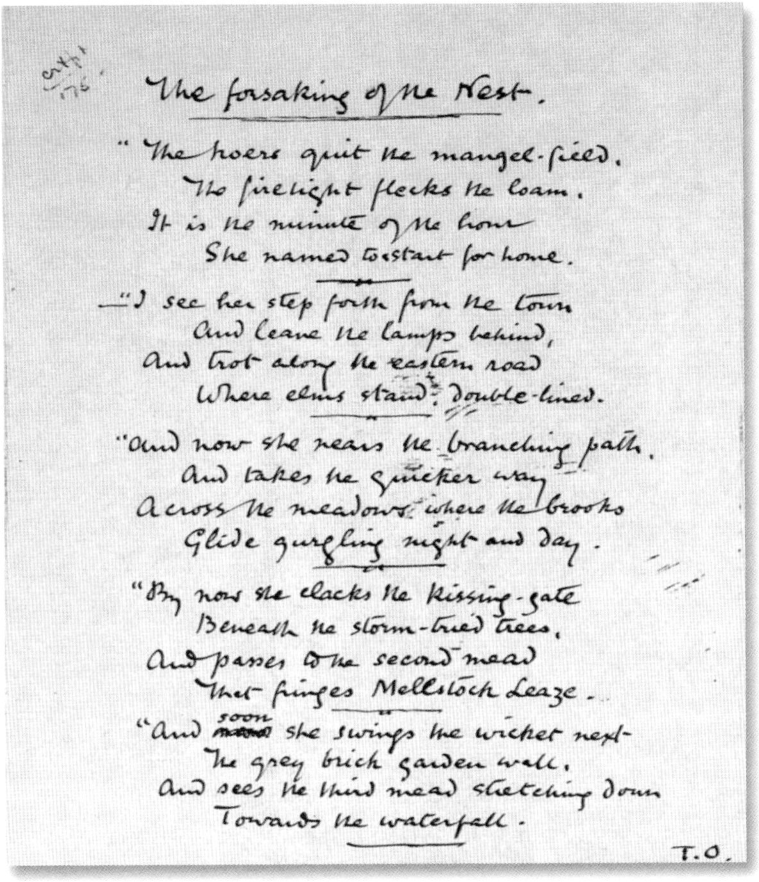

The forsaking of the Nest.

"The hoers quit the mangel-field.
The firelight flecks the loam.
It is the minute of the hour
She named to start for home.

"I see her step forth from the town
And leave the lamps behind,
And trot along the eastern road
Where elms stand double-lined.

"And now she nears the branching path.
And takes the quicker way
Across the meadows where the brooks
Glide gurgling night and day.

"By now she clacks the kissing-gate
Beneath the storm-tried trees,
And passes to the second mead
That fringes Mellstock Leaze.

"And soon she swings the wicket next
The grey brick garden wall,
And sees the third mead stretching down
Towards the waterfall.

T.O.

FAR LEFT A collection of letters by Hardy

LEFT A script by Thomas Hardy

Chapter 6

Celebrating Hardy

Criticism varied considerably for Hardy's work both in his novels and his poems which could probably have resulted from his style. Many considered that he had "lapses" where prose and verse were not as carefully executed, however, in his autobiography, Hardy himself explains that these moments were intended and were not carelessness or incompetence on his part. Furthermore, his subject matter was perpetually criticised for its openness that love was purely about sex, and marriage an unhappy institution. But, the author was not appreciative of these thoughts and critiques and was particularly frustrated that his works were often described as gloomy or macabre. He especially didn't approve of the word "pessimism" being applied to his writing. But whatever the critics had to say, Hardy enjoyed a highly productive career as both novelist and poet.

Many of the author's former notebooks were destroyed, however, those that remain show his intellectual growth and development. But, much of what Hardy was will remain unknown, for the highly prolific author was extremely reticent, almost secretive and even when he was 86 and visited Hardy Cottage in order to talk about maintaining the garden he was keen for further shrubs, trees and other foliage to be added to the property in order to keep the house and its surroundings more private. Despite being attributed as the author of Hardy's two biographies, more commonly known as *The Life, The Early Life Of Thomas Hardy*, published in

ABOVE Thomas Hardy receives the freedom of his home town of Dorchester, 15th November 1910

1928 and *The Later Years Of Thomas Hardy* published two years later in 1930, were actually written for the most part by the author himself and Florence Dugdale Hardy in effect only wrote four chapters of the two volumes and added other additional material at a later date.

It isn't just scholars and students who are interested in Hardy today, despite what some critics may think however, as he is still much revered among the readers of the "classics" and enchants and entertains through his poetry and prose in much the same way as he did at the turn of the 19th century.

CLASSIC LITERATURE

LEFT The Prince
of Wales surveys the
gardens at Hardy's
cottage in Dorset.

CLASSIC LITERATURE

ALSO AVAILABLE:

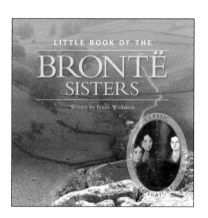

Available from all major stockists

The pictures in this book were provided courtesy of the following:

GETTY IMAGES
101 Bayham Street, London NW1 0AG

SHUTTERSTOCK
www.shutterstock.com

Creative Director: Kevin Gardner

Design and Artwork: David Wildish

Picture research: Ellie Charleston

Published by Green Umbrella Publishing

Publishers: Jules Gammond and Vanessa Gardner

Written by Emily Wollaston

CLASSIC LITERATURE